The only way to fulfil a dream is to plant the seed, nourish and nurture it, and watch it grow...

Dreams are for living...

First published in 2002

Revised and reprinted 2003.

by Billet Doux Design co., Orchard House, Coney Weston, BURY ST EDMUNDS, Suffolk IP31 1HG

Tel: 01359 221421 email: liz@cowlingfloristry.freeserve.co.uk

Floristry: Claire Cowling ICSF MSF Tel: 07949 442213 and Liz Cowling NDSF FSF

Photography: Peter Griffin, GGS Ltd., Norwich, Norfolk. Tel 01603 622500

Sketches: Lizzy Jackson, Bury St Edmunds, Suffolk

Origination & Layout: Ben Cowling & Liz Cowling

Print: Reflex Litho, Thetford, Norfolk. Tel: 01842 754600

A catalogue record for this book is available from the British library.

BRIDAL FLORISTRY FOR THE 21st CENTURY

straight from the heart

Claire Cowling ICSF MSF
Liz Cowling NDSF FSF

THE LANGUAGE OF FLOWERS

There is a language little known,
Lovers claim it as their own
It's symbols smile upon the land,
Wrought by Nature's wondrous hand;
And in their silent beauty speak,
Of life, and joy, to those who seek
For Love divine and sunny hours
In the language of the flowers.

Anon

CONTENTS

INTRODUCTION

Never before has there been such an exciting time to be a florist... and weddings are one of the major areas where artistic ability and flair can be wholly indulged, exploited and enjoyed. We have a vast world full of amazing natural materials all readily, and quickly, available to us - whether from the other side of the world or outside our own back door. Bridal fashion has never been so diverse and challenging, nor venues so varied. Flowers can become the most sensual accessory or the biggest nightmare of the day. It just depends how they're used!!

Exciting, inspiring, commercial floristry is achievable. Fine workmanship, sound product knowledge, wide open eyes and an enquiring, inquisitive mind coupled with the courage to experiment and the patience to master new techniques and develop ideas give us a greater understanding of our subject. At the same time it gives us not only confidence but also satisfies our own creative ability and the 'perceived value' of the finished work.

We like to take some of the materials that nature provides for us and use them in a sensitive way to create bridal designs that are suitable for a wide range of brides, bridal gowns, seasons, levels of expertise, overall wedding theme and, of course, budget. By keeping a wide-open mind and honing our skills we have all we need to create beautiful bouquets. Good technique should never be underestimated, it can make the difference between an exquisite and mediocre piece of work. It is possible to weave emotion and feeling into designs, make them sophisticated or casual, dirt cheap or horrendously expensive. The beauty of the flowers may be transient and short, but the memory that they can leave is indelible and lives on indefinitely.

It is necessary to make lots of considerations before choosing wedding flowers. These considerations are all linked and play a vitally important part in selecting the right type of bouquet and flowers for the personality of the bride to complement the gown and the style and size of the wedding as a whole.

Personally, we feel that the design of the bridal bouquet is determined only in part by the bridal outfit; it's style, colour and overall volume. It is essential to know in detail the style, colour texture of fabric of the outfit. A sketch, picture, or ideally, a photograph of the prospective bride wearing the gown, will make it much easier to imagine the final effect and help determine the most suitable shapes and size for the bouquet. At this stage ascertain whether the bride has any personal preferences, colour in mind, likes and dislikes. Ascertain whether the bouquet is to be symbolic and incorporate hidden meaning. Consider the bride's personality, her age, size and style preferences; traditional, avant garde, simple, country, sophisticated, adventurous. Think flower types, texture, form, colour scheme. Consider the kind of colour scheme suggested, how materials will inter-relate. Think about fabric and dress materials, patterns and shapes. Consider the season, adding warmth and cosiness to a winter design or coolness to a summer piece.

Time was when church or registry office was the only option, and everything far more straightforward.   Consider the overall theme for the day, and it's venue. The time of year, the availability of suggested materials and their costs (especially if out of season). Take into account the scale of the ceremony and celebration.

Select flowers which will stand up to what is required of them for the duration of the occasion. It is important to consider the overall weight of the bouquet, so the bride can feel comfortable if wanting to hold the flowers for a long period. Show how and where the bouquet is to be held.

A beautiful bridal bouquet needn't cost a fortune, nor necessarily take hours and hours to make, but it should touch the soul and be an indelible reminder of a perfect day.

Our definition of a good florist... one who can savour the beauty of Nature all around us, gather a little of it, then, with the skill in the fingertips, work a little magic on it - and share it.

Tantalise the senses... nestled in a sisal collar or aluminium wire framework these bridal posies may be in soft and sensual colourings, yet ooze style and are very twenty first century. Lots of texture and fine detail. Roses... carnations... matricaria... gypsophila... hypericum... Hand tied and traditionally wired, and decorated with intricate beadwork and sheer ribbons.

sensual
sensual
sensual
sensual

13

Using 'Prado' carnations as the focal flower, a quartet of posies decorated in different ways show limitless possibilities with this favourite form. Texture is important. marguerites... ranunculus... gypsophila... chrysanthemum... roses... all sit happily alongside the frilly form of softly coloured green carnations, bugle beads and cord. Dreamy, seductive and perfect for both brides and attendants.

daisy

feminine and transparent... a cylindrical form which is graceful and certain to be a huge success for anyone who craves something a little bit different. Easy to carry and beautiful to look at, the design is fashioned on a hand made wire mesh base and decorated with sisal, skeleton-ized leaves and choice flower material. Zantedeschia, Dendrobium orchid florets, rose buds. Rolled and strung rose petals add fine detail and interest.

delicate and ethereal in cool white and clear green, the design would be fun and stunning in vibrant, clashing colours or soft, romantic pastels...

beautiful baroque

RETRO

anemones

cascading

[T]he rose...

the flower of love, gently fashioned into a single huge bloom.

Classic, yet oozing with style, sophistication and twenty first

century appeal. Teasingly framed in a cheeky feather collar,

the Carmen rose bouquet is a perfect design for lots of styles

of bridal gown. Dewdrop beads catch the light.

evocative

sensual

evocative

Marabou feathers and a cascading floral ribbon decorate a cosy, warm muff for winter wedding celebrations. Gorgeous to look at and oh so cosy...

Alternatively, a shield shaped bouquet packed with tantalising textures. Soft, downy feathers, fluffy hare's tails (Lagurus ovatus), opaque Honesty discs (Lunaria annua), Ornithogalum arabicum, sisal and pearls...

Think tactile... feel the warmth. Feathers, fur, soft materials, creamy whites, loads of textures, lots of shapes.

winter

winter

27

A single chrysanthemum bloom decorated with fine trails of Ceropegia woodii, berries and pearls is surrounded by a Marabou boa collar. Play with textures and soft, teasing colours...

Think romance, countryside, meadows, warm sunshine. Vary the theme, contrast solid lines with cascading Tillandsia usenoides, and flowers of simple form. Keep colours sharp and vibrant.

I ♥ U

and don't you forget it!

Suggestive and secretive. Semi transparent, hinting at a love of the countryside and woodland, whilst still enjoying a hint of sophistication. Loads of contrasting textures, tactile mosses, fluffy feathers, fine Cymbidium orchids, shiny leaves, gnarled and knobbly twigs. All combine to make an unashamedly romantic bouquet full of secrets and memories.

Marguerite

Fresh as a daisy. Light to hold and very twenty first century. A smart posy shape brought bang up to date using only Marguerites, bear grass and pearls strung on long lengths of fine decorative wire. Continue the simple retro theme throughout; decorate the tables with huge bowls of daisies tied plainly with wide tulle bands, huge satin bows, or gingham ribbons.

TANTALISING
TEXTURES

love is...

A pair of choice Phalaenopsis orchids, gorgeous glass beads and soft downy feathers link together in this transparent and ethereal posy.

Zantedeschia and rolled rose petals create a sheaf style bouquet with an ultra modern twist...

Zantedeschia

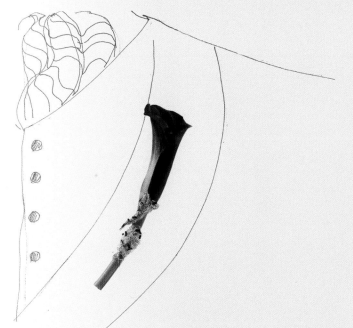

Passion Flowers !!!

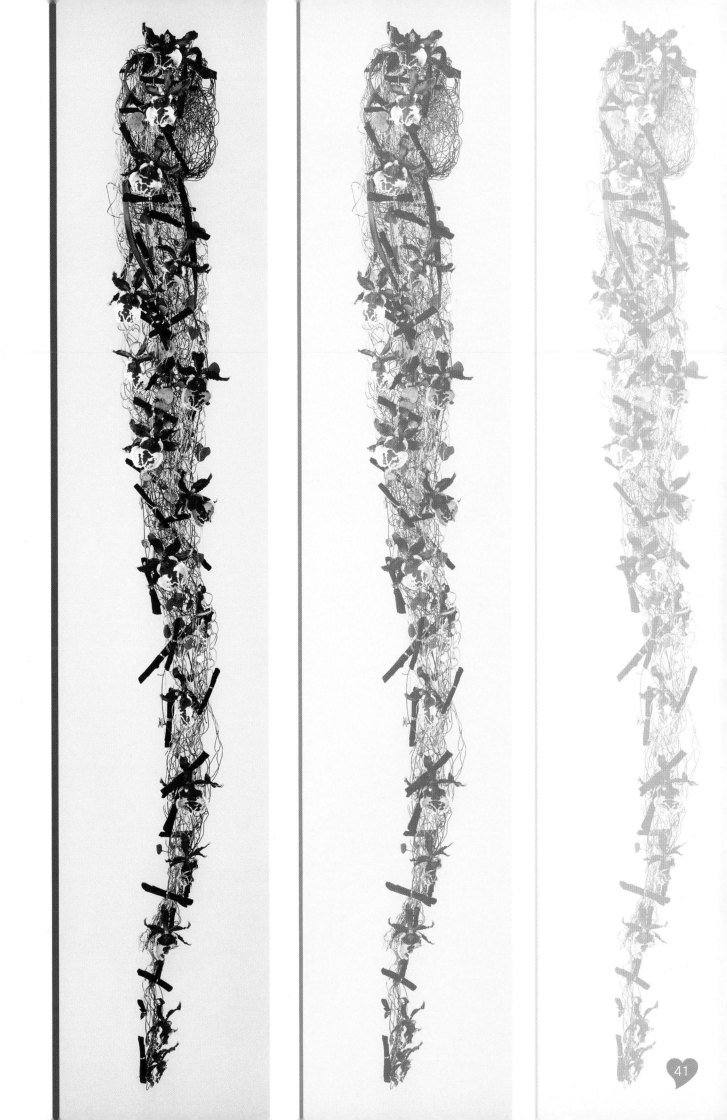

CORNUCOPIA

CORNUCOPIA

TRANSPARENT

passionate red

Rich, passionate red... beautiful roses enclosed in a Marabou collar and suggestive lace trimmed with sequins and beads... or a medley of different coloured red roses and deep red carnations in a tightly grouped handtied bouquet.

Simply irresistible

*V*elvety, luxurious, rich red 'Black Baccara' roses cocooned in an intricately decorated framework of Muehlenbeckia, grasses, coral fern and beads.

Hearts and Roses

St. Valentine's...

*E*very wedding is a truly special occasion, but why not incorporate meaningful shapes or materials into the design when planning a Valentine's or Christmas wedding to make it even more memorable?

*F*or the Valentine's bride a heart, for the Christmas bride, holly leaves, berries and winter evergreens

Christmas...

Cheerful, happy colour combinations in these hand tied posies in various grouped styles. Make your bouquet as individual as you by carefully choosing the flowers like jewels. Absolutely perfect for a spring or autumn nuptial.

NEW CLASSICS

Traditional styles, new interpretations.
Twenty first century bouquets for thoroughly modern brides...

AUTUMN

Dare to be different. Stand apart from the crowd. Choose distinctive flowers arranged in an innovative way. Make the buzzword for the day 'FUN.' Sunny, cheerful yellows will make the day go with a swing... whatever the weather outside... choose contrasting forms and textures. Craspedia, tiny orchids, carnation petals...

and HIP
FUNKY

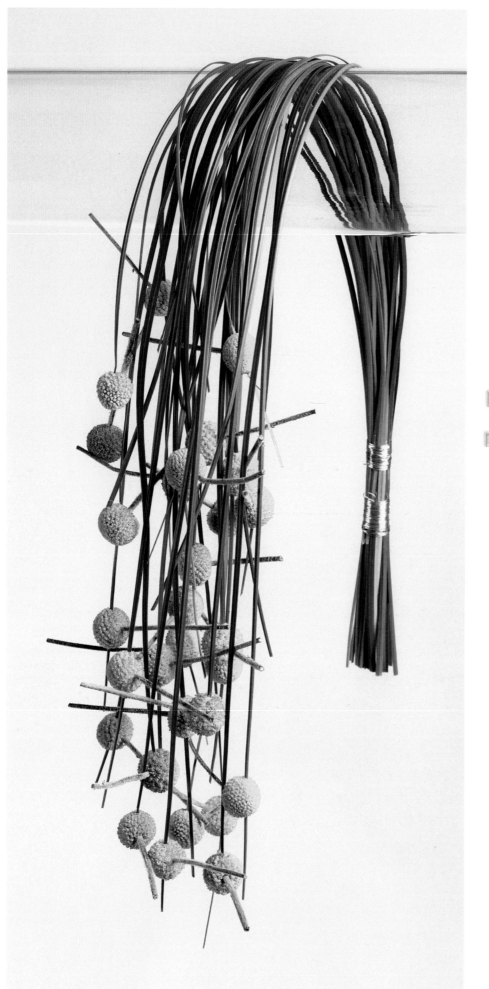

craspedia

ORCHIDS AND BERRIES

Gloriosa

Gorgeous to look at, easy to carry. A selection of special flower material and berries fashioned into a casual, country style hand tied bouquet. A hand made heart adds interest and brings an extra touch of romance to the design. Perfect for any time of the year, and any type of ceremony.

the language of flowers

roses for love, pansies for thoughts... choose flowers with meaningful sentiments like the Victorians. The rose is the flower of love. According to legend it was created by the gods and remains the most popular of flowers. Red rose for true love, white rose for purity and spiritual love.   Folklore has it that carrying pansies with you ensures the love of your sweetheart. There are many more to choose from - forget me nots (true love), jasmine (grace and elegance), honeysuckle (sweetness of disposition), lily (purity) and chrysanthemum (I love).

roses
pansies

HYDRANGEA

cornucopia

73

decadent roses
decadent roses

*P*erfectly formed, building on nature,

A dozen or so roses fashioned into one

huge Carmen rose. Softly coloured,

exquisitely formed, decorated with

vines and beads. Good roses to use are

Vendela, Black Baccara, Naranja.

bridal arch

sophistication

imagine

paradise

the day is for two, starting out in life together... a pair of roses nestle together symbolically in a Galax leaf cone, surrounded by groups of other roses, and masses of hydrangea and gypsophila. Casual, in style and easy to carry. For the groom a boutonniere of gypsophila cocooned in another Galax leaf cone, and topped with a golden heart.

just the 2 of us...

Million Stars

$\mathcal{M}$illion Stars gypsophila makes a dreamy, romantic bouquet. The perfect flower around which to theme the whole wedding's floral arrangements. Make huge gypsophila topiaries finished with enormous tulle bows. For the tables make massed gypsophila wreaths and garlands . Scatter semi-dried hydrangea florets on the tables. $\mathcal{S}$imply achieved, a fairy tale effect...

A bouquet to nonchalantly swing whilst walking up the aisle. Thoroughly modern and extremely light and easy to carry, this design is a dream come true. Transparent glass beads threaded onto bear grass glisten like dewdrops.

Chic, modern and lots of fun...

Avant gardé, and very twenty first century.

Based on the quintessentially English posy

shape and the classic Carmen rose, this

bouquet is structured so as to be hexagonal in

form, providing a contrast to the central flower.

Lots of textures jostle over, under and through

the framework. Skeleton band pearls, grasses.

Up to the minute design and easy to carry. A bridal ribbon which slips casually over the wrist and cascades gently is a stunning alternative to a traditional bouquet. Full of several layers of exciting and unusual flower material, and complemented by tiny Marabou feathers the design is sure to be admired.

The classic teardrop shape bouquet is given a new twist with a tight central posy of gypsophila, decorated with a long tail of grasses, beads and long trails of flower heads.

Phalaenopsis orchids teamed with sweet smelling Stephanotis and freesia make a classic English style bridal bouquet, perfect for most styles of gowns. White, soft cream and cool greens are perennial favourites. For boutonnieres use single orchids framed by a few choice flowers. Perfect...

haute

$\mathcal{H}$eld like a sceptre, a simple massed design finished with a single choice orchid, and lots of fine detail makes a really special yet different bridal bouquet.

$\mathcal{A}$n avant garde design slips over the wrist and arches gracefully. Zantedeschia, long dainty garlands of gypsophila and Senecio rowleyanus follow the form of the aluminium framework.

avant garde

A large shield shaped bouquet, light and easy to carry, high on style. A few choice Phalaenopsis orchids decorate a haphazard framework of grasses. Long strings of threaded florets and beads cascade down through the work. Transparent glass beads catch the light and glisten in the sunshine...

A large bouquet with masses of impact and feeling,

using a single choice chrysanthemum bloom as the focal

flower. Soft, seductive colouring, and gorgeous textures

throughout. Pearls add the final finishing flourish.

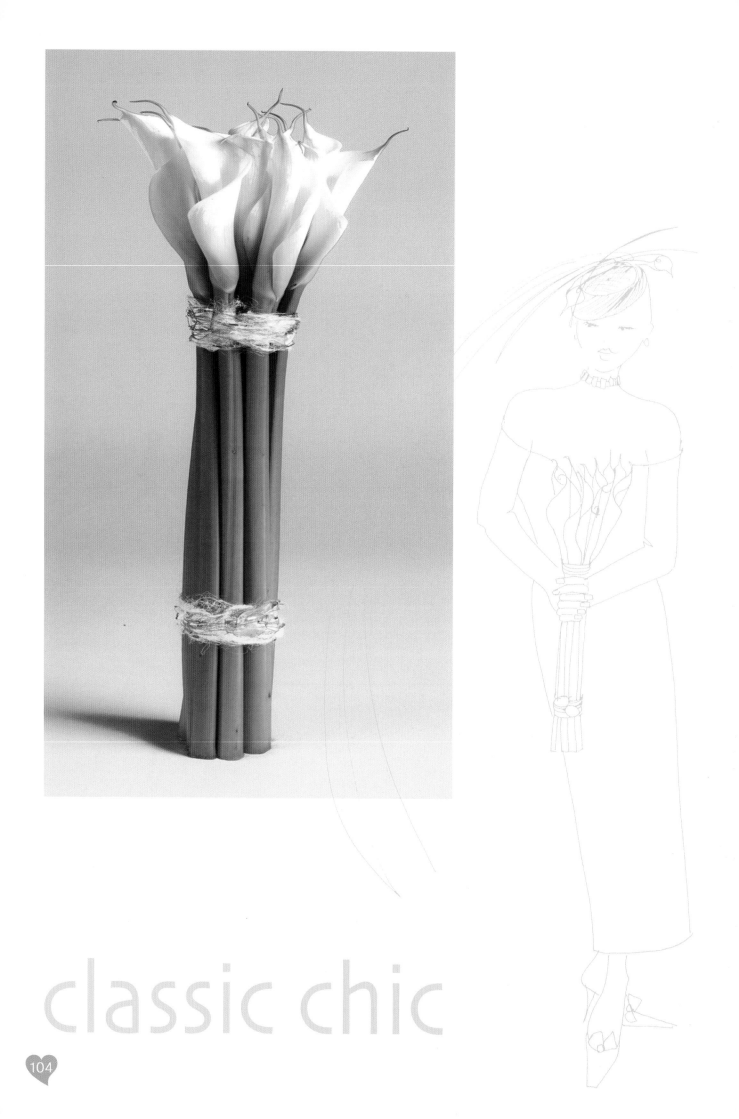

classic chic

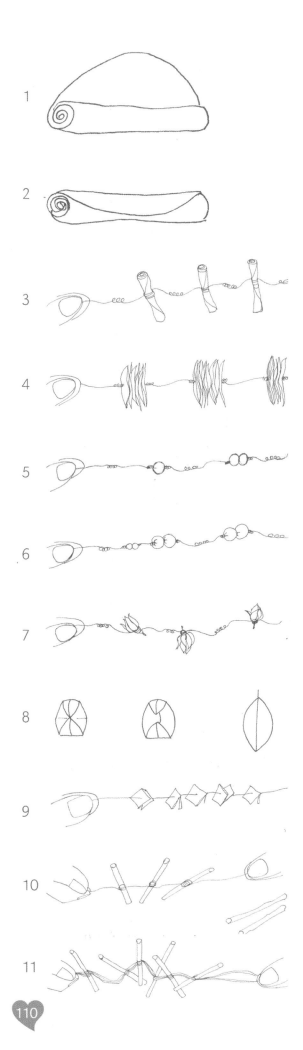

THREADING TECHNIQUES

Rose petals are useful to use in a variety of ways. Individually rolled, then wired on to a fine gauge reel wire (see sketches 1, 2 & 3), they are stunning woven through work. Stacked (see sketch 4) they make beautiful features, or if made into long tassels provide an interesting design feature. The wire used should be of a fine gauge, and a small loop made so that the petals do not slide. When the stack is large enough again make a loop to secure, or fasten a bead. This technique is also perfect for leaves such as Eucalyptus, Euonymus, Myrtle etc.

Small berries such as Hypericum are good to thread and make easy, effective additions to work. Use fine beading wire, pierce berry through the centre and thread onto wire, vary distances between berries. Make a tendril effect by twisting wire between berries around either a piece of stalk or heavy stub wire. (See sketches 5 & 6). Immature roses are also effective in strings (sketch 7).

Geometric forms are often effective. This effect may be achieved with leaves, rose petals or other suitably shaped material. Fold leaves as shown in sketch 8, folding first ends to the centre, then sides to the centre. Fold once more in half, then thread onto beading wire (sketch 9). Secure with loop.

Sticks are another useful addition. Cut into lengths of either the same or varying lengths. Cornus and deckreed are good to use. Bind tightly about four times with fine beading wire then give a twist for added security. Continue adding sticks until the desired length is achieved (sketch 10). Twist lengths of sticks together when used for 'tails' (sketch 11).

HAND-MADE WIRE MESH

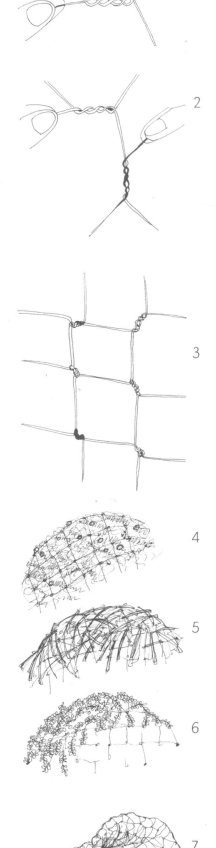

1

2

3

Hand-made wire mesh is useful for a wide variety of applications in a many different styles of work. Once the technique is mastered it is quick and easy to make and forms a base for things as diverse as boutonnieres, to cornucopias and dresses. Ensure that the gauge of stub wire used is suitable for the finished article, whilst the framework needs to be strong, it rarely needs to be totally rigid. Weight is a further consideration, therefore, use as light a gauge wire as possible. To begin, twist two lengths of stub wire simultaneously (sketches 1 & 2). Add further lengths to each end (sketch 3). It does not matter if the mesh is not symmetrical, Ensure that all the edge wires are twisted in so they do not snag. Once the shape has been formed, it can be decorated with skeletonized leaves, bullion wire, linen watten, sisal, bear grass, lavender etc. See sketches 4, 5 6 & 7.

4

5

6

7

8

ABSTRACT SHAPES

Often it is exciting and appropriate to use abstract shapes as the basis for transparent, rather avant garde style designs. The frames for these may be made from fine gauge welding wire bent into shape. For the funnel shaped design (sketch 8), the top and bottom have been formed from taped stub wire which has been bound with decorative reel wire then bent to the required size. The longer wire is then attached. Finally, a cord handle is fixed to the top, which then leaves a shape perfect for decorating with skeletonized leaves, bullion wire, sisal etc. Similar techniques have been used with the balloon shape (sketch 9).

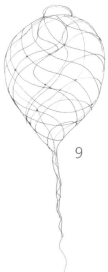

9

DECORATIVE COLLARS

1

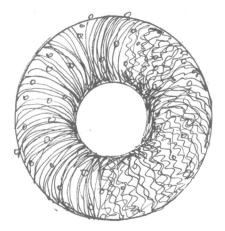

Decorative collars are easy to make, and add distinction to a simple bouquet. They are also something that may be made well in advance and are easy to store.

Cut a circle of thinnish card to the required size. Cut out a hole in the centre. Cover as required with sisal, or leaves, or a mixture of sisal, feathers and bullion. Attach four stout stub wires so that the frame may be held firmly when being used. Other useful covering materials are linen watten, fine, clean flat moss, skeletonized leaves. Flat faced flowers like pansies and violas are good for decorative purposes, as are lavender and rosemary. See sketches 1 to 3

2

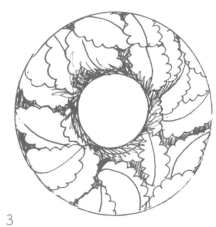

4

3

HANDLES

In the past, handles have been simply finished off with a satin ribbon, but it is easy to give them some distinction often in a much quicker and simpler fashion than ribboning, and certainly more fashionable and in keeping with the bridal design. Finely teased out sisal may be bound tightly on to the handle for a fast effective finish, as may cleaned, dry flat moss. Feathers can be held upside down and bound tightly to continue design features, as may fountain grass (see sketch 4), or steel grass. Other mediums may be cord, large leaves or fine straight stems. Handles for hand-tied bouquets are also important design features, and it is vitally important that they are the correct length for balance, comfort and ease of handling, as well as being perfectly clean of leaves, thorns etc. They may be finished off simply with a ribbon or length of tulle to compliment,

CARMEN ROSES

Carmen roses, once mastered, are classic centrepieces that may be used for decorating in several ways. Make stub wire hairpins in three different lengths ie 1cm, 1.5cm and 2cm using a fairly fine gauge of wire. Take a perfect, tight rosebud and wire through the calyx with a sturdy stub wire (sketch 1), remove sepals and any inferior petals. Carefully remove petals from around fifteen open roses. Retain seedboxes for use in other designs. Make sure that only perfect petals are used, add individually to the bud, using smaller petals to the centre and larger towards the outside. Pin through toward the base of the petal and overlap the next petal (see sketch 2), continuing until the required size is achieved. Ensure that small pins are used to the centre and larger towards the outside for extra security. Check the profile all the time (sketch 3). When complete tape the stem, which may be left long or short, depending on the final detail added. This could be a framework of vine, beading etc, or left simple and classic by backing with several large leaves.

'Prado' carnations, Vendela rose, Matricaria, Hypericum 'Honey',' Eucalyptus 'Baby Blue,' sisal, fine hand made wire mesh and beads.

Bloom chrysanthemum, 'Bianca' roses, Matricaria, Hypericum 'Green Flair,' Gypsophila, Senecio rowleyanus, aluminium wire, fine organza ribbon, sisal.

A quartet of posies, various materials; 'Prado' carnations, Matricaria, Marguerites,''Bianca' & 'Vendela' roses, Gypsophila, pine needles, sisal, aluminium wire, Eucalyptus 'Baby Blue,' Hypericum 'Honey,'cord & beads

'Prado' carnations, 'Vendela' roses, Hypericum 'Honey,' steel grass, Gypsophila, Viburnum tinus, Brunia albiflora, Matricaria.

Marguerites, Gypsophila, Nerine flexuosa, Panicum fountain, Hedera, decorative grasses, organza ribbon.

Zantedeschia, 'Viviane' spray roses, Dendrobium orchids, Ornithogalum arabicum, sisal, cords and bullion wire.

'Prado' carnations, Cornus alba, Asparagus setaceus, Panicum, Grevillea robusta, Hydrangea macrophylla, steel grass.

'Prado' carnations, Asparagus setaceus, spray roses, Hedera, steel grass, bear grass, sequins.

Ranunculus, Ornithogalum arabicum, Arum, Phalaenopsis, pine needles, Viburnum opulus 'Roseum',' Brunia albiflora, Eucalyptus 'Baby Blue,' bear grass, skeleton band, Tillandsia usenoides.

'Vendela' roses - approx one dozen, feather collar, dewdrop beads, decorative cord.

Dendrobium orchids, 'Bianca' rose petals rolled, green Physalis alkekengi, Hedera leaves & berries, sisal, Marabou feather trim, skeleton leaves, pine needles.

Lunaria annua, Ornithogalum arabicum, lichen moss, Vanda roots, Lagurus ovatus, Skeleton band, Cornus, Steel grass, Hedera,- leaves and berries, pussy willow, pearls.

Bloom chrysanthemum, Hedera leaves and berries, steel grass, Senecio herreianus, Ceropegia woodii, Marabou feathers.

Marguerites, Ranunculus, Hypericum 'Honey,' Snowdrops, Tillandsia usenoides, Senecio rowleyanus, Hedera, steel grass, Viburnum opulus 'Roseum.'

Spray roses, Zantedeschia, Physalis, Cymbidium orchids, Senecio rowleyanus, moss, Hydrangea, Marabou feathers, Hedera, a piece of branch.

'Bianca' roses, Stephanotis, 'Prado' carnations, 'Viviane' spray roses, Viburnum tinus, Asparagus setaceus, bear grass, Panicum fountain, long feathers.

'White Lydia' spray roses, Matricaria, sisal, pearls and tiny hearts.

Deep red willow, deck reed, Black Baccara roses, Ophiopogon nigrescens, Viburnum berries, Marabou feathers.

Phalaenopsis orchids, Ophio-pogon planiscapus nigrescens, Senecio rowleyanus, rolled rose petals, Willow, Marabou feath-ers, various beads

Zantedeschia, steel grass, willow, Ceropegia woodii, pine needles.

Oncidium orchids, 'Black Baccara' roses - rolled petals, Ceropegia woodii, lots of coloured wire.

Physalis, 'Jacaranda' roses, Ama-ranthus caudatus, Antirrhinium, Grevillea robusta, Panicum foun-tain, Clematis vine, bear grass, Lunaria annua discs (outer cases)

Symphoricarpos albus, Callas, Clematis vine, roses, freesia, Panicum, Galax leaves, bear grass, Asparagus setaceus, Hedera, sisal, fine organza ribbon.

Ornithogalum arabicum, Pussy willow, Red willow, Phalaenopsis orchids.

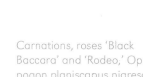

'First red' roses, Cornus, moss, Salix udensis 'Sekka,' Cerope-gia woodii, length of lace, beads.

Carnations, roses 'Black Baccara' and 'Rodeo,' Ophio-pogon planiscapus nigrescens, Aspidistra elatior.

'Black Baccara' roses, bear grass, 'Tamango' spray roses, coral fern (Gleichenia polypodi-odes, various vines and beads.

'Jacaranda' roses, Amaranthus caudatus, Sedum, Hydrangea, Sandersonia, Panicum, Galax, Asparagus setaceus, Marabou feathers, bear grass, aluminium wire.

'Passion' roses, Hedera, Cerope-gia woodii, moss, piece of lichened branch, Muehlenbeckia vine.

'Sacha' roses, Ilex - berries and leaves, Cornus, Hedera - berries and leaves, Hebe.

Viburnum berries, Physalis, Rosehips, Alstroemeria, Pansies, Dahlia, Hypericum berries, Senecio herreianus, steel grass, bear grass, Amaranthus cauda-tus, aluminium wire, various vines, wire heart.

Willow, tulips, carnations, 'Black Beauty' roses, ranunculus, Hyper-icum, Viburnum tinus berries, Brunia albiflora, Asparagus den-siflorus, bear grass.

Sunny colours, roses, tulips, carnations, ranunculus, Hypericum, bear grass, Brunia albiflora, steel grass, Eucalyptus.

Roses, Typha grass, Rhipsalis and beads.

Roses - standard & spray, Craspedia, carnations, chrysanthemum, ranunculus, Hypericum, Rhipsalis, Eucalyptus 'Baby Blue,'

Tequila roses teamed with sunny yellow roses, steel grass and textured ribbon.

Willow, ranunculus, Asparagus densiflorus, Viburnum opulus, carnations, tulips, albiflora, Hypericum, bear grass, Typha, Eucalyptus.

Ilex berries, Grevillea robusta, Vanda orchids, rose petals and seedheads and steel grass.

Craspedia, Oncidium orchids, carnations, Senecio rowleyanus, rose petals, bear grass, Panicum fountain

Vanda orchids, Ilex berries, Cornus and bear grass.

Gloriosa and Zantedeschia.

Hydrangea, various garden type roses, Celosia argentea, Hypericum, Rowan berries, Clematis vine, Hedera, wire heart.

'Blue Gene' roses, pansies, lavender, Lunaria annua, sisal and organza ribbon.

Hydrangea, sisal, sequins.

'Metallina' roses, hydrangea, bear grass, vines, beads and organza ribbon.

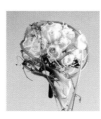

Around a dozen 'Vendela' roses, various vines, linen watten, bear grass and beads.

Zantedeschia, Eucalyptus berries, leaves and pods, Miscanthus sinensis variegatus, Matricaria, sisal and beads.

'Akito' roses, Zantedeschia, Senecio rowleyanus; Passiflora vine.

 Roses, Dendrobium orchids, Senecio herrieanus, Panicum fountain, Lunaria annua, sisal and tropical shell

 Tropical shells, oriental lilies, outer cases of Lunaria annua, Panicum fountain, bear grass, moss

 Gypsophila paniculata, 'Eskimo' roses, Hydrangea macrophylla, Galax leaves and fine organza ribbon.

 Gypsophila paniculata 'Million Stars,' Hydrangea macrophylla, Euonymus, soft coloured cord and organza ribbon

 Dendrobium orchids, bear grass and clear glass beads.

 Around a dozen 'Vendela' roses, steel grass, Lagurus ovatus, skeleton band, sisal, pearls.

 Ornithogalum arabicum, Dendrobium orchids, 'Prado' carnations, Hypericum 'Green Flair,' steel grass, sisal and Marabou feathers

 Gypsophila paniculata 'Million Stars,' roses, Ornithogalum arabicum, 'Prado' carnations, steel grass, Typha grass.

 Dendrobium orchids, Physalis, Skeletonised leaves, bear grass, Hedera, Asparagus setaceus, small hearts and aluminium wire for frame.

Phalaenopsis orchids, 'Akito' roses, freesia, Stephanotis floribunda, Jasmine officiale, Myrtle, heather, grasses

 Phalaenopsis orchids, Nerine flexuosa alba, bear grass, Senecio herreianus, steel grass, clear glass beads

 Gypsophila paniculata 'Million Stars,' Phalaenopsis orchid and Ornithogalum arabicum.

 Gypsophila paniculata 'Million stars,' Zantedeschia, Stephanotis floribunda, Senecio rowleyanus, Tillandsia, aluminium wire

 Spray roses, Phalaenopsis orchids, Antirrhinium, Nerine flexuosa alba, Gypsophila paniculata 'Million Stars,' Senecio herreianus, steel grass

 Bloom chrysanthemum, deck reed, linen watten and pearls

 Arums, Stephanotis floribunda, Ornithogalum arabicum, Symphoricarpos alba, Antirrhinium, Hedera, Asparagus setaceus, Larch, Birch and Viburnum.

CHRYSANTHEMUM FRUTESCENS
Marguerite

A flower of simple form suggesting innocence, romance and countryside. The strongly branched daisy shaped blooms are just perfect for country hand ties, 60's retro designs as well as designer works. First cultivated in England in 1699, it is a real 'traditional' English country

flower. Available as a cut flower throughout most of the winter, and also in spring and summer as pot plants & standard lollipops; making the perfect and effortless link to venue decor. Works especially well with other country flowers such as Convallaria majalis (lily of the valley), Myosotis (forget me nots), roses, Gypsophila and Centuarea (cornflowers).

CONVALLARIA MAJALIS
lily of the valley

This wonderfully scented little flower has long been associated with bridal work and it's easy to see why... ethereal, delicate, pure &

clean in form... available, on root, all year through. Used to best effect in traditional & simple works, where it's fragile beauty may be appreciated to the full. Perfect partner to Stephanotis, Phalaenopsis and roses. Look out for the extra special pink variety. For stunning table centres pot up several plants and decorate with sisal - pure luxury and perfect for giving afterwards...
Pot up the roots & wrap nicely, to give as a token to the brides mother, and be planted later as a lasting reminder of a special day.

DENDRANTHEMA
chrysanthemum

Although not a naturally thought of material for fine bridal work, these are truly beautiful flowers just perfect for so many design ideas. Have a distinctive, autumnal scent, are inexpensive and easy to condition and use. Not to be written off and listed as passé.
Lasts for ages without

water and available in a fantastic range of colours and form. The large incurved blooms make the centrepiece to a bouquet in one go, which may be decorated in a huge variety of ways. The small flowers of spray varieties may be threaded and strung into long lengths. They look stunning in cascading trails, alternatively use petals of large blooms individually, and randomly glued.

DIANTHUS
carnation

Not the 'dated' and old fashioned flower some would have us believe, but a superb and exciting flower to use for a variety of reasons. Makes a quick base for a retro posy, requiring only detailed decoration to make a really 'wow' bouquet. Adds gorgeous texture to a hand tied, individual petals

strung into long lengths or glued on to designer pieces look simply wonderful. Short lengths of stem bound onto long lengths of decorative reel wire and twisted together to make gorgeous trails and tails. Carnations are inexpensive, available in a huge array of colours, are long lasting and easy to condition. Keep away from over mature flowers or fruit as sensitive to ethylene.

FILLERS

Necessary to cover mechanics and add volume to bouquets. Loads of choice of materials in this category. Ammi majus, Trachelium (especially white!) wax flower, Alchemilla mollis, Aster ericoides, (September), Hypericum, Limonium (some varieties, in moderation). Kalanchoe, Hydrangea and Celosia are also exciting to use - recess

deeply or clustered in dense groups, to highlight focal and main flowers. Important to choose texture, form and colour carefully for best effect. Good filler foliage includes Hebe in various varieties and colours, Rosmarinus officinalis (Rosemary), Myrtus Communis (Myrtle), and especially when in flower or berried, various Viburnums V. tinus, V. opulus 'Roseum', or V. opulus 'Compactum') and many varieties of the Eucalyptus family such as 'Baby Blue.'

FINE LEAVES & GRASSES

This is an exciting list that could go on forever and ever... versatile materials like Xerophyllum tenax (bear grass), Xanthorrhoea australis (steel grass), Equisetum (snake grass). Others could include Miscanthus sinensis variegatus (China grass), Typhus latiflolia

(typha), Ophiopogon planiscapus 'Nigrescens,' Gleichenia polypodiodes (coral fern), Asparagus asparagoides (smilax) and Asparagus setaceus. Each have a huge range of potential uses in bridal floristry. Use as a flourish, to cover hand made mesh bases (bear grass), to make long trails, use to emphasize form and add distinction. Cut steel grass into short lengths, bind onto decorative reel wire and make long trails to bind around and over designs. Twist together several to make a distinctive tail. A few leaves of O.planiscapus 'Nigrescens' are perfect to add the 'wow' factor to a simple Phalaenopsis corsage.

FOLIAGE GENERALLY

Essential. Not necessarily used in great wedges, but used sparingly and sensitively, can add a whole new dimension to the bridal design. Leaves threaded into long strands can make a fine feature in a bouquet (try Eucalyptus, Euonymus or Hedera), cover bases or collars with leaves for interest (good ones for this include Stachys lanata, Hedera, the reverse side of Eleagnus, Viburnum). Use more traditionally as a filler to the flower material.

Eucalyptus, Hebe, various Viburnums, Hedera. Don't disregard dried autumnal leaves, these add good texture especially for bases trails.

FUN & FUNKY

In this category there are many unusual treats. Craspedia, Conkers, Celosia argentea 'Cristata' (cockscomb), Heliconia, Anthurium, Eryngium... all lend themselves to being used in exiting and distinctive ways. Craspedia are beautiful threaded or speared onto steel grass. Celosia in it's distinctive colourings and unusual

forms are gorgeous for something out of the ordinary and teamed with other unusual materials - Anthurium maybe? Use grouped tightly and deeply recessed. Dismantle Heleconia to use in small sections for a new slant to a bouquets. Use colour and texture in a dramatic way.

GYPSOPHILA PANICULATA

One of the most versatile flowers around for wedding work, looking romantic and sensual if used well. The name is derived from the Greek 'gypsos' meaning chalk, and 'philein' which means 'to love.' Available throughout the year with an

ever increasing number of varieties. Used en masse it provides the perfect base for decorating with beads, cords, threaded florets and leaves. Cut into small sections and wire closely (garlanding method) onto decorative reel wire to make flowery tails and trails. Relatively inexpensive, it's useful to theme the whole occasion around the flower using huge bows of tulle to embellish Gypsophila topiaries. Lasts well when conditioned properly.

LEAVES

Leaves, used singly, stacked, layered, curled or framing a piece of work can make all the difference. Consider effect required. Need to be the correct size, colour, texture, form and scale to be wholly effective. Shiny, furry, variegated, veiny, feathery. Each will give a vastly

different effect to the overall design. Favourites include many varieties of Hedera, Galax viceolata, Aspidistra elatior, Fatsia and Cordyline. Hedera can be layered, stacked on lengths of decorative wire, used as a neatener on bouquet backs, used to cover collars or individually. Aspidistra are good for distinction, but be careful of over dominance.

LILIES

Not a particular personal favourite but a very important group of wedding flowers. I prefer to see them used in a simple posy shape or a very traditional bouquet. As stems are usually multi flowered it is much easier to wire and tape individual flowers before assembling to give greater control to the

design. If a hand tied effect is required, use wired flowers to the centre and natural stems toward the outside, thereby enclosing the wired part of the bouquet. Finish neatly with a ribbon. Condition carefully with cut flower food at half strength for best results. Remove stamens to eliminate risk of staining clothes

MEANINGFUL MATERIALS

The language of flowers may be very appropriate for use in bridal flowers. Things that readily spring to mind are roses - for love, ivy - for fidelity, corn - for riches, rosemary - remembrance, forget me not - true love. It

is wise to use considerable tact before mentioning too much folklore, as flowers may be equally disregarded as unlucky!!! It is best to keep to safe ground, unless specifically asked...

MOSSY BITS

Mmmm.... wonderful softly coloured long trails of fresh Tillandsia usenoides, a hundred times better to use than the dried. Use flat moss to cover pieces of exposed foam or to cover collars or muff frames. Make sure all little bits of debris are removed. Make tiny spheres and hearts of moss and bind tightly with

reel wire. Use Indian or Spanish moss as an additional texture. Avoid dyed mosses, as colours may run if moistened.

NATURAL BEADS

Semi precious and glass beads are gorgeous to use but Mother Nature also provides a fabulous range of natural beads for us to use. Favourites include

Senecio rowleyanus and is a 'must have' for wedding work. It is easy to look after and produces long strings of natural beads, Senecio herreianus is also available - the difference being that the beads are elongated rather than round. Hypericum is perfect for threading onto decorative wire. Use close together or apart. Stack Lunaria outer discs for a tassel effect or wire individual transparent discs for an ethereal look. Experiment with other types of berries as available. Check that non-poisonous before putting them in young children's bouquets.

ORCHIDS

Such a wide and diverse group of flower material, and so perfect for bridal work. Phalaenopsis the beautiful moth orchid - has to be one of the favourites - making any design special and luxurious. Use on the natural stem for simple bouquets. Selectively remove a few individual flowers to make a little finer and easier to use (use for buttonholes or corsages). Add as a final flourish. Use in haute couture stye bouquets, bind a small piece of dampened cotton wool to the end of the stem before taping and using.

Spray lightly with Chrysal Glory or similar. Dendrobium if used well are excellent, last wonderfully. Vandas, Miltonia or Paphlipedulum use as the focal flowers. Gorgeous. Vanda roots are also wonderful to use as an added texture - fantastic colour and very pliable, brilliant to work through designs.

ORNITHOGALUM ARABICUM

A very useful pure white flower with a distinctive black ovary perfect to dismantle or use as a base texture (minus the open flowers).

Single florets are perfect for threading onto long strings of decorative work, their distinctive black centres add to their appeal. Buy in early as these often take a few days to open enough to use. Long lasting at least 14-21 days. Keep in shallow water in preference to deep water.

PIPS

Not actually 'pips!' but 'pipped flower material.' Several gorgeous things come into this heading, and are perfect to use. Hyacinth, Stephanotis, Sandersonia, Physalis, Hoya, Bougainvillaea, Hydrangeas.

Use threaded into long tassels for use in designs, spaced along lengths of decorative reel wire interspersed with beads. Wire Hyacinth or Stephanotis individually using a pearl on the hair pinned wire to add distinction. Hydrangea florets (choose well matured florets) add an exciting dimension to the simplest of bouquets. Also useful are the preserved florets in pure white and biscuit colour, very ethereal and delicate.

RANUNCULUS ASIATICUS

These beautiful simple shaped flowers with their many layers of fine, papery petals in clear jewel colours are a wonderful flower to use in bridal floristry. Best used in simple posies. Originating from the eastern

Mediterranean they are most widely available during the winter and spring, although they are available all year. A perfect flower to base a whole wedding theme on - simple posies, table centres of massed Ranunculus in terracotta pots and finished with moss and huge pots or urns filled similarly. Stylish, colourful, special yet easy. Condition carefully, using cut flower food.

ROSES

These have to be the most well loved flower of all times, and not just for weddings. Poets have written about them since time immemorial, lovers give them as tokens of affection. what could be more appropriate? Choose the type, size, form, colour and variety carefully for best effect. Scent may also be a deciding factor - the evocative perfume of Jacaranda or Ecstasy for example. The range of roses now available commercially is so vast that we are only

limited by the limitations of our imaginations.
Use simply, in a massed hand tied, dismantle and reassemble as a classic Carmen rose, thread, or roll... use the seed head as a design feature. Tiny Italian roses are perfect for detailed work. Varieties such as Vendela, perfect for Carmen roses, ensure the roses to be used are fully mature. Condition carefully, using cut flower food.

STICKS & THINGS

Mikado sticks (deck reed), twigs, Cornus, Corylus, Salix, lichened branches, Bamboo all are useful and easy to use. Mikado sticks

are currently very popular and are perfect to use as a delicate base material. May also be bundled and wired onto decorative wires, wired individually then spaced out along wires and twisted together. Similarly Cornus and Salix give a similar but much heavier effect. Lichened branches give a romantic, woodland feel to designs.

TULIPS

A perennial favourite. Hundreds of varieties, forms and colours to choose from. Perfect for simple hand-tieds, and designer pieces. Long stemmed French tulips are gorgeous for weaving through and

around bouquets. Parrot tulips, with their irresistible colour combinations and fascinating formation are exquisite on their own. Best used seasonally, although available all year. Ensure the customer understands their limitations and doesn't expect them to stand without water for long periods. Another perfect flower to theme a wedding around, using only one kind of material.

VIBURNUM

A huge family which gives us some wonderful materials to use. V. opulus 'Roseum' - guelder rose - is a perfect colour, it's clear green globes of simple shaped flowers blend well with most colour combinations.

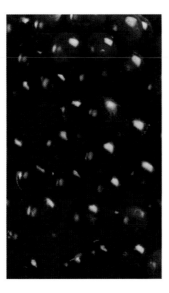

Condition carefully in lukewarm water, and use special flower food for best results, available most readily December through to May. Viburnum tinus is great as a filler foliage both plain, when in flower or berried, depending on season. The ovoid berries are gorgeous colours and perfect for threading onto decorative reel wire. V. opulus 'Compactum' - sold primarily for it's glossy, bright red berries throughout the autumn, these are best used in heavy clusters. Add form colour and texture to autumnal bridal work.

VINES & TRAILS

Masses of choice, colour and texture again. Wisteria, Muehlenbeckia, Convolvulus (bindweed), Rubus, Cereopegia woodii, Senecio rowleyanus, Clematis, Asparagus asparagoides (smilax)... all have a valued place. Select carefully, taking into consideration the final effect required - whether it is to create a collar or add a gentle flourish. Consider the colour and texture of the stems,

whether they are woody, knobbly, clean, shiny. Take off some - or all - leaves if too many. Asparagus asparagoides, is the most gorgeous trailing material to use in romantic, long cascading bouquets. Bindweed is beautiful to use stripped of all foliage, and has the added bonus of being free. Can often be found with the stems twisted tightly round each other. Fabulous.

ZANTEDESCHIA
Calla

Funnel shaped, elegant and of simple form. Stunning flowers. Zantedeschia are favourites for all kinds of bridal work and available in a fair range of sizes and colours, including the almost black variety. Available most of the year, perfect for Calla wands, as well as a host of design ideas. Essential to choose the correct size, both in

terms of head size, length and stem thickness. Excellent for limited bouquets, over-arm sheaf style bouquets and in modern or where manipulation shows the stem to full advantage. Leave out of water for easy manipulation in designer works. If using large headed stems for a Calla wand, it may be preferable to wire the central couple of flowers to reduce the overall bulk and width of the finished stems.

THE DAISY

I'd choose to be a daisy,

If I might be a flower:

Closing my petals softly

At twilight's quiet hour:

And waking in the morning,

When falls the early dew,

To welcome Heaven's bright sunshine

And Heaven's bright tear drops too.

Anon

ACKNOWLEDGEMENTS

Life has to be a bit of an adventure - we're only here a limited time after all. And dreams are for living. Who would have thought that so soon after dipping our toes into the world of publishing that we'd need to revise and update our first book? The success of the project is not only ours, huge thank you's are due to Lizzy Jackson for the fabulous sketches - the book wouldn't have been the same without them; to Peter Griffin at GGS for the wonderful photography and all at Reflex Litho who have been involved in the printing process. Their input and attention to detail has ensured that this, the finished article, is just what we hoped for.

Thanks also to Jane and Rachel for their invaluable help and comments, and the family for putting up with the inevitable mayhem whilst the project has been taking shape and invading almost every waking moment!!

The biggest thanks this time around - from both of us , must go to Ben - aged 15 - who's now on his third book! Ben has laid out all the pages in this new edition and it's been a pleasure as well as great fun to work with him and see the pages taking shape. Lots of love and huge thanks. The added bonus this time around for Ben is being able to see the printing process right through to it's conclusion, as his work experience week's coincide with the printing. Enjoy, Ben, and special thanks Richard for organizing it.

We hope you will be able to gain pleasure, inspiration and profit from our combined efforts. Dreams can come true, but only if you believe they can, and really, really want them to.

'Thank you' from both of us - straight from the heart.

BIBLIOGRAPHY

The Royal Horticultural Society Gardeners' Encyclopedia of Plants & Flowers 1991

Snijbloemen - Aalsmeer 1990

Flower Council of Holland

Foliage for Florists - Veronika Strong 1996

Decorative Cut Flowers - Coen Gelein & Nees Joore - 1988

The House Plant Expert - Dr D G Hessayon - 1999

INDEX